The Great Book
How to Feel Great

It is my hope that this book takes you on that great voyage of self-discovery that will help you uncover your hidden treasures. Treasures that will help you live the life you were meant to live and become the person you were born to be.

Make your mark in this world.

Leave something significant after you are gone.

Share your gifts with the others.

Be happy with your best efforts.

And remember everyone else is doing their best.

How To Feel Great

From the beginning of time people all over the world have been searching for a method that will have the ability to make them feel great and confident.

When we feel great, we are happy and when we feel confident, we feel strong and safe. After all, confidence is just a feeling that sends a message to the brain that we are capable and have the resources to carry out a task or overcome an obstacle.

This satisfies our core human need for survival.

Who wouldn't want to feel great all the time?

The mistake most people make though is that they are looking in the wrong place.

Almost everyone believes that something that will allow them the ability to feel great is outside themselves.

"If I had what you had I would be happier".

"If I had a stronger body, better physic, more friends, more money, a bigger house, a bigger car, more sun, then I would feel better".

"If only I was a champion, I would feel great". "If only more people liked me."

The fact is though, all these "wants" only build an illusion that feeling great is something external and something outside of our personal power to access.

Of course, we should all work at achieving a better life and there is nothing wrong with enjoying new experiences through cars, gadgets, holidays and winning competitions, life after all is about experiences.

The truth, though, is that the ability to feel great is something we must access from within ourselves and once we learn to access this ability to feel great every day. It can be a source of personal power that we possess for the rest of our lives that will help us feel safe, value ourselves more, make better decisions and develop into that best version of ourselves.

Can such a priceless skill be achieved?

Could such a skill that will replace feelings that suppress a humans' quality of life such as low self-worth, insecurity and a life half lived really exist?

This book is to give you this power to feel great when you feel that you need to, without any external stimulants or gadgets.

I will describe the process that I have devised through my own experience of 30 years of working with a range of individuals and groups ranging from elite athletes, performing artists and leaders in business to those who live a life through a cloud of darkness, despair and blind to ever experiencing a happy future.

Some of you reading this book may fit into the first category, some of you will fit into the last category and some of you will fall in between.

It doesn't really matter where you are in life, what you do, where you live or who you believe you are, we all have the right to feel great. For it is only when we feel great that we can perceive and even achieve great things in our future.

When I say great things, that can be a great mother, father, brother, sister, builder, athlete, doctor or just a great friend to others. Too often now we are put under the pressure of being high achievers in all walks of life under the illusion that you must have achieved great things to feel great.

Before we start though I would like you to make a promise. Not to me, but to yourself.

Promise yourself you will read this book often and practice the process I am teaching you.

You are unique and have been put on this planet for a purpose. You may not be aware of this purpose but through the practice of these techniques it will present itself to you.

Remember, it is vitally important to follow the instructions specifically and to be aware of how you feel, where you feel the emotions and what thoughts are generated with each feeling.

The Process

Every day in every city and town around the globe humans begin their day in a similar fashion. They wake up and make their way to the bathroom.

In every bathroom there is a mirror in which they look at their morning reflection.

This Mirror will be your feedback tool for the process I am about to teach you.

I want you to go right now to a mirror and observe your image. Record in a book or diary what you are focusing on as you look at your reflection in the mirror.

Do you focus on what you do not like about your reflection?
What would you like to change if you could?
What do you believe is out of place?
How do you "feel" overall about your image?

Give yourself a score for each of these questions ranging from 1 to 10.

How much do you love that image?

How inspired do you feel when you look at your reflection?

How much do you believe in that person looking back at you?

If your total score for these questions was 15 or less, you will be glad you invested in this book.

I am now going to take you through my process for feeling great every day.

Each letter that makes up the word "GREAT "is a reminder and step of the powerful process that I am about to teach you.

This process will not give you anything externally to make you feel great but will release the greatness you already possess inside yourself.

Let us begin.

G

The best thing about the letter G is that it stands for Gratitude.

Gratitude is not just a great word, but such a powerful human emotion. In fact, it is probably the greatest human emotion.

You see when we experience the vibration of Gratitude through our nervous system it causes what is known as coherence. (The quality of forming a unified whole)

If there is one word you should add to your vocabulary today, tomorrow or soon, it is coherence. All the research shows that when you have it, your life can be so much better than when you don't. Add coherence to your personal vocabulary, learn how to practice it and experience the benefits within yourself and your daily living.

Coherence is the state when the heart, mind and emotions are in energetic alignment and cooperation. The HeartMath Institute Research Director Dr. Rollin McCraty says. "It is a state that builds resilience – personal energy is accumulated, not wasted – leaving more energy to manifest intentions and harmonious outcomes."

Dr McCraty and others have conducted studies that show a particularly effective method of achieving coherence that's user-friendly and helps replace negative emotions with positive ones - emotion self-regulation.

So how do we generate this powerful feeling of gratitude?

First, let us look in the mirror.

Now I would like you to ask yourself a question.

"What, not who, is that looking back at me?"

Let us explore what is looking back at you in the mirror. That reflection you are observing in the mirror is a phenomenal mechanism that takes in around 11 million bits of information through the senses to send to the brain for processing every second! How awesome is that?

This body is a phenomenal healing machine that maintains itself. If you cut the skin and broke the bones it would begin to work on healing and rebuilding right away with the objective of making itself even stronger for the future.

You can increase the physical strength, endurance speed and balance of this body by a simple process of daily practice if you choose. The only limit on that is the one you wish to put on it. Other humans have taken their body and trained it to lift cars, swim oceans, run faster than some animals and perform the intricate skills of a monkey on bars and Olympic rings.

Even if some humans through trauma, neglect or misguidance abuse this phenomenal machine they can rectify it once more through support, guidance and a new focus that will bring it back to optimal functioning.

A great example of this was Tyson Furey the heavyweight boxing world champion who through a mental health issue gained 8 stone and overindulged in alcohol and prescription drugs.

He made the decision to get back on the right path through the right support and training. He took off the 8 stone, got back in shape and regained the heavyweight world title once more.

A phenomenal achievement and an example to us all that this phenomenal machine we walk about in, can achieve what our mind can set as a goal.

Take your time and think about that until you come to the realisation that you are awesome because you walk about and

11

live in this highly sophisticated and intelligent body. Now look closely at those eyes in your reflection.

Behind those eyes lies a human brain. The brain is performing trillions of tasks every second. Taking in phenomenal amounts of information that must make sense. The brain is one of the most powerful computers in the universe. It is estimated we have approximately neurons, that is about 166 times the number of people on the planet.

1. Humans continue to make new neurons throughout life in response to mental activity.

2. Each neuron connects with, on average, 40,000 synapses. (Chemical receptor gaps between nerve cells).

3. A piece of brain tissue the size of a grain of sand contains 100,000 neurons and 1 billion synapses all communicating with each other.

4. All brain cells are not alike. There are as many as 10,000 specific types of neurons in the brain.

5. Neurons send information to your brain at more than 150 miles (241 kilometres) per hour.

6. All neurons lined side by side would stretch 1000 km.

Close your eyes and think of how powerful that is, feel that power in your head and then open your eyes to observe your reflection once again.

Before moving on to the second stage of the process familiarise yourself with this feeling of self-awesomeness.

Feel that gratitude for all these functions plus many more that allow you to enjoy the variety of experiences in your life.

These functions that happen unconsciously within this mini universe we call the body that many of us take for granted.

Keep looking at your reflection until this feeling of gratitude manifests from within your body.

R

Resources.

As you continue to observe this body in your reflection that is performing these awesome functions, ask yourself "what skills and resources has this body learnt, practiced and mastered up until this present moment in my life?

Now begin to remind yourself of the human skills that you have learnt over your lifetime.

The thousands of hours, days, weeks, months and years of practice in the many physical and analytical skills we all learn growing up.

From learning to talk, walk, feed ourselves, get dressed, brush our teeth, run, climb, dance, sing, ride bicycles, roller-skate, skip, play sports, musical instruments, reading, writing, arithmetic as well as all the many subjects in school as well as college, university, driving, career skills and parenting skills if you are that far on in your life journey.

Let these amazing facts with the memories flood back into your memory bringing that sense of achievements with them.
Wow!!! How powerful and skilful are you?

Now before we move on, notice how you feel now with your eyes closed and familiarise yourself with these feelings inside.

Where do the feelings house themselves in your human body?
How do they affect your breathing patterns and your internal voice? Keep looking at your reflection in the mirror with this sense of achievement and self-confidence.

E

E stands for Emotional intelligence.

Out of all the human skills we have an option to learn, I would have to say in my opinion that emotional intelligence is very important.

As humans we tend to feel before we think in many circumstances and experiences that we get involved in.

I believe that this has been built in as a survival mechanism. Every emotion we feel carries with it a message to the brain.

When a human feels depression they are experiencing the lowest vibration on the scale, and it carries the message "I cannot help myself and no one can help me."

When they experience grief after a loss, they receive the message "I cannot help myself, but I am open to others helping me."

Fear is a very common emotion with its message of "Back off and be careful, danger or discomfort ahead."

Then we have another very common emotion, Anger! Anger carries the message of something is not fair, I have been wronged in some way"
Some of the more positive emotions we experience are Courage, Acceptance and Confidence.

Courage

Courage is that energy we release when we decide to move forward even in the face of danger. To step up and out of our comfort zone.

This is usually for the sake of others. For example, if you are nervous about water and have slight anxiety and fear about jumping into a river this fear would be quickly overcome by courage if you witnessed a young child falling into a river and was in distress. Before you had time to think you would move forward to save that child's life.

A similar circumstance we hear of is people entering burning buildings to save others trapped inside at no thought of their own safety.

Courage is an emotion we all possess, like all emotions it will never be gained outside yourself.

Acceptance

This is a feeling that there is no need to change anything about ourselves, others, or the world we live in. Everything is OK how it is. Sadly, many people go through life craving acceptance from other people in life and will adjust their behaviours, looks, and even take up hobbies that they have no passion for just to gain this acceptance from others.

The sad fact is though, that we do not need to gain the feeling of acceptance from anyone but ourselves and when we begin to understand how to release these emotions, we can access them any time we wish.

Confidence
Confidence like every other feeling we experience has a message and a process that will cause it to manifest.

Its message is "I am capable!"

So how do we know we are capable? Where do we install this belief that we can do?

Well, how do we install this feeling of belief and confidence in a team or individual that we have great belief in?

Well, if you think about this, we usually study the individual and familiarise ourselves with their past achievements, skills, and resources until this feeling we call a belief has evidence to back it up. This is part of the process I am taking you through in the mirror exercise so that you can develop this feeling of self-belief when you gaze at your own reflection.

Now to make this clear for you, we need to understand that emotions are only energy in motion running through the nervous system. The energy will run from a low to high frequency and we then give it a label.

The good thing is though that we can only experience one feeling at a time. We cannot feel hot and cold at the same time, no more than we can feel happy and sad at the same time.

So, if you find that your vibration aka emotional state is low, simply turn up the frequency, practicing replacing what you do not want to experience instead of resisting it and giving it all your focus.

So now when you have completed the first 3 exercises in the mirror observe what emotion you are experiencing now as you stare at your image.

A

A stands for **Affirm.**

Affirmation: The action or process of affirming something.

There have been many books written about affirmations to change one's thinking, health and behaviours.

I have observed many and believe many have been written without much personal practice or experience behind the material.

The mainstream method is to keep repeating what it is you would like to experience.

This method usually takes a long time and can be very disheartening for the practitioner.

As an example, if you wish to lose weight and are told to affirm over and over "I am thin" or "I am my ideal weight" there will be a feeling of disbelief to accompany this accompanied by a voice saying "No you are not."

This is basically because every feeling we experience carries with it a message for the brain.

If we are feeling cold, the message is "put more clothes on", "turn on the heating." Or "find shelter."

If we are feeling fear the message is "back off and be careful."

If we feel a statement is not true because the feeling of belief is not there, then the message is usually "No I am not."

I have been teaching the art of affirmations for over 20 years and it is in the third stage of my empowerment program for a reason, not the first stage.

The feeling must match the affirmation, or the subconscious mind will not accept it.

The subconscious mind is around 88% of your total mind and is very intuitive to feelings.

Therefore, up to now I have been taking you through a process that is designed to invoke powerful feelings from facts and memories about yourself.

All you need to start doing now is to describe specifically what you are feeling.

These affirmations will have a magnifying effect on your feelings and make them even more powerful.

Never repeat affirmations around what you do not want or how you do not wish to feel. The sub conscious mind does not understand negatives. When you state I do not have to carry excess weight on my body, or I will not eat chocolate anymore, all it hears is I will carry excess weight on my body, or I will eat chocolate.

So, keep affirming specifically how you feel physically and emotionally after putting the 4 exercises together as you gaze at your reflection in the mirror.

If you feel physically stronger repeat "I feel strong, my arms, my legs and my body feels strong, because I am strong. My mind is strong and I am strong because I am ...." (State your name here.)

Begin to build momentum on this as the energy and affirmations will match and begin to magnify these feelings.

"Not only am I strong, I am powerful, I walk about in this phenomenal human body, this healing machine that masters many skills driven by my awesome human brain" Then let your own mind give you it's own affirmations. Write them down as your own to repeat because they were born from you, so they will not feel like a lie when you repeat them.

Now compare how you feel now as to how you felt before you began the exercises and take note.

T

T is for **time**. There is an old saying that time is a great healer. It can heal physical wounds and even lessen the effect of fall outs with loved ones and friends. It is a double-edged sword though with also the ability to decay the body over time and multiply the anxiety of emotional trauma and fears.

We are only given so much time every day and for many of us only so much time to live our aspirations and gain experience in this life.

Some of you reading this believe that you have all the time in the world and many of you will always feel that you are running out of time to get things done.

Whatever you feel will become your reality because time is truly subjective.

The most important fact about time though is to remember that the amount of practice you put into it is very important.
The GREAT process is no different from any other skill you wish to master in your life.

It takes practice. And the amount of time that you put into your practice will reflect on the results that you receive.
Therefore, I suggest that every time you look at your reflection in a mirror practice this process.

At first it may seem amusing or just small. But so does the tiny seed from an oak tree. But just like the seed from the oak tree, it has massive resources and potential sitting dormant and waiting to grow.
Water that seed of great potential that lies within you by practicing this process every day.

Self Discovery

Now you have received my process for empowering the mind for feelings of greatness, you can take the time to get to know yourself better and find more clarity on the direction you should be going towards your goals in life.

This chapter is filled with snippets of knowledge and questionnaires designed to weed out any doubt about your great abilities and to help water those seeds of self-belief in your mind. Seeds that will grow into massive trees of personal power.

As with any journey, your journey of personal success and achievement must start with a destination in mind.

The vision of what you want and where you wish to be in the future.

Setting goals is a fundamental component to long-term success. The basic reason for this is that you can't get where you are trying to go until you clearly define where that is.

Research studies show a direct link between goals and enhanced performance in life. Goals help you focus and allocate your time and resources efficiently, and they can keep you motivated when you feel like giving up.

Just before we head off though on your journey , let us unload some of the extra baggage that you may be carrying that may hold you back. Many people have been inspired to achieve a goal of some sort in the past only to be put off by others judging their performance or breaking down under stress and pressure due to a lack of self belief in being able to cope with challenges along the way.

So let us look at some of the obstacles that may hold you back from progressing towards your aspirations and goals in life.

The Fear Of Them

When you have a need for approval from other people around you, this means that you value the beliefs, opinions and needs of others above your own. Their opinion of you can become far more important to you than your own view of yourself. Receiving disapproval becomes a painful experience. Your entire decision-making processes are eventually taken over by your need for the approval of others. You cannot take any decisive action without their approval. You sacrifice your own dreams and ambitions in order to have their approval.

Amongst the negative consequences of approval seeking behaviour are:

- Lack of achievement.
- Lack of personal fulfilment.
- Low self-esteem and confidence levels.
- Reduced performance.
- Increased stress.

You may argue that you do not engage in approval seeking behaviour. However, there are common behaviours which you may fail to recognise as approval seeking. Sometimes these behaviours are used as a tactical compromise, to keep the peace, or because the situation is not really that important to you. In some instances, as long as they are not too frequent, it may be useful to allow others to have their way. However, when these behaviours occur too frequently, or are motivated solely by a need for approval, you are adopting an unhealthy behaviour which can lead to severe problems.

Approval Seeking Behaviours

The following are some of the most common approval seeking behaviours:

- Changing or softening your position because someone appears to disapprove of your behaviour.
- Feeling upset, worried, or insulted when someone disagrees with your opinion or suggestions.
- Expressing agreement (verbally or non-verbally) when you do not agree with someone.
- Doing something which you do not want to do because you are afraid to say 'No'
- Spreading bad news and gossip to gain attention.
- Consistently apologising for your words and deeds whether others have expressed disapproval or not e.g. 'I'm sorry but...'
- Pretending to be knowledgeable or an authority on a subject because you are afraid to admit that there is something you do not know.
- Attempting to coax people into paying you compliments and/or getting upset when they fail to do so.

Any behaviour which is contrary to your identity and purpose, or conflicts with your core beliefs, is generally done to gain the approval of someone else.

You are entitled to your own thoughts, beliefs, and opinions. Just because you think differently to someone else it does not mean that one of you is right and one of you is wrong. It is important to be able to respect the right of others to have their own opinion but to do so; you must first be able to respect your right to have your own opinion. Respecting your own views requires you to avoid approval seeking behaviours.

The biggest irony with approval-seeking behaviour is that it usually produces the opposite results to those which are intended.

If you take a moment to consider those people whom you respect most, you will find that one of their strongest traits is their ability to be true to who they are. They will always stand up for what they believe in.

Approval seeking behaviour is intended to get more approval and respect from others, yet what people generally respect is the very opposite i.e. people who are true to themselves. It is nice to have the approval of others but the way to get it is to have self-approval and self-respect. While modern life conditions people to seek approval; familiarising yourself with the approval seeking behaviours, listed above, will help you to identify when you are seeking approval, allowing you to take corrective action.

Reducing Anxiety And Stress

If the signs of anxiety at an important event are becoming too much for you it means that negative arousal has developed. Breathing will be faster; legs will feel heavy and shake and you may not be able to think straight. Sleep may also be difficult, especially the night before the event.

You may not get enough hours, and if that is not bad enough, the hours you do get may not be as deep as desired either. In those cases, the anxiety must be reduced. Many find that reading or listening to audio's on visualisations work well.

Instead of thinking about what might happen, lie down and slowly relax your body and mind. The room may be darkened while the body is relaxed, starting from the extremities and slowly extending up to the centre of the body.

Your audio's for relaxation, soft music or breathing exercises should be practiced or listened to during this time so that the ultimate result is lowered heart rate and breathing rates, resulting in better sleep.

Another treatment is massage. A long, slow full-body session will lower anxiety as well on an ongoing basis, perhaps weekly. These more frequent massages cut anxiety and release body toxins.

Thought Redirection

Another way to tame pre-performance jitters is to think of something else. Many young athletes, artists and entrepreneurs take little books such as this or my "The forgotten secret for success" book along to important events with them to replace negative thoughts with inspiring and motivational ideas about themselves.

Breathing Exercises

Breathing exercises have been a part of many cultures promoting health and well being for centuries. When one is under stress they tend to breathe very shallowly and starve the body of vital oxygen.

An example of a simple but effective breathing exercise:

1. Take a slow breath in through the nose (for about 4 seconds)
2. Hold your breath for 1 or 2 seconds.
3. Exhale slowly through the mouth (over about 4 seconds)
4. Wait 2-3 seconds before taking another breath (5-7 seconds for teenagers)
5. Repeat for at least 5 to 10 breaths

Many times the feelings of anxiety we feel before a performance can remind us of previous times in our life when we experienced something that made us feel anxious afterwards.

This has the effect of fooling us into it happening again in the present moment or the future.

The best way to deal with this is to get rid of those bad memories and stop them repeating themselves over and over again.

Here is an example of such an exercise

Exercise for Removing Bad Memories

So, is there a memory that keeps forcing itself into your mind's attention, and makes you feel bad?

Well, as you think about that memory now, with your eyes closed, notice that the image or movie of the memory in your mind has a location in space.

Is the image directly in front of you? Is it to the right? Or to the left?

Now attempt to move the picture towards you slightly then back into its usual position. Have you noticed that you can reposition the picture?

Well now imagine in front of you a giant slingshot.

And notice the picture sitting in the centre of the slingshot if it is a movie place the TV in there.

Pull it back and feel the tension in the elastic build in your mind and body as you stretch it all the way back, and let it go with a loud twang.

Now watch the picture shoot off until it's just a dot in the distance.

Think about something else for a moment such as what you ate last, then think of the memory again.

Is it in its original position or has it moved?

Pull out your slingshot again and give it another go.

Keep doing this until the memory has no effect on your state at all and stays a dot in the distance when you think of it.

In my mind I keep a trash can and when I have a memory that is really annoying me I imagine it on a piece of paper, then reach out and scrunch it up, before dropping it into the trash can to my left with a satisfying crash.

I wonder which ways you can imagine trashing and re-editing those old videos you call negative memories?

Keeping a Promise

Have you ever had the experience of a friend or family member breaking a promise they made to you?

Maybe you were promised that you would be taken somewhere special like a big game or a party and were let down at the last minute or forgotten about.

How does this make you feel when this happens?

If people keep breaking promises to us we eventually begin to distrust them. This actually has the same effect when we break promises to ourselves.

How many times have you made a promise to yourself that you would practice a specific skill that could enhance your performance in a chosen field? And then find an excuse that would prevent you from carrying out that extra practice.

Maybe you even made a promise to put in extra revision for academic work, or help your parents or a friend more. And then once again found an excuse to let yourself down.

If we keep breaking promises to ourselves that we have made, then we eventually come to the same conclusion as we came to with others who broke numerous promises. That we cannot rely on ourselves!

We should treat the promises that we make to ourselves just as importantly as those we have made to close friends. When we keep promises to ourselves we begin to trust ourselves.

Start your promises with some small tasks that will help you feel better about yourself and build self-trust. Never make big promises that you feel will be hard to keep!

Some small examples are:

- I promise to read over and study my work 30 extra minutes each day.
- I promise to practice my new physical skills 30 minutes each morning and evening.
- I promise to look for opportunities to help my parents or a friend each day.

What small promises can you think of would help you become a better person?

I promise...

I promise...

I promise...

The Saboteur

Self Criticism

Never, ever criticise yourself along your journey.

If you develop a habit of criticising yourself and suggesting that you are not a good person, there is the danger that through time you may actually believe it.

Many people in life never achieve anything in their life because they believe deep down they are not worth achieving or owning anything that will make them feel good.

1. Accept that you are a human, a member of the human race. We all make mistakes. This is why they put an eraser on top of a pencil!
2. Realise that if you do not love and accept yourself, it will be almost impossible to accept love or friendship from anyone, as you won't believe that you deserve it.
3. Distance yourself from any critical thoughts that arise in your mind. Just step back and notice them while choosing to take action in the direction of things that you believe will make your life better.
4. Decide that you will appreciate yourself for your efforts and for what you have already achieved. Commit to staying focused on what is important to you and on what you wish to accomplish
5. Realise that self-criticism does not improve performance. It just makes you feel bad and may even hinder your making the changes you wish to make that will make you a better person.
6. Break down any large goals into manageable pieces. Focus on what the obstacles are and what it will take to overcome them.
7. Realise that success often involves failing first and learning from mistakes.
8. Decide to be the best you can be rather than comparing

yourself to others.
9. Forgive yourself if necessary and move on.
10. Focus on what you can control rather than the things you can't control.

Where Are You Going?

Now that we have got rid of some of that unwanted baggage and have fuelled up the vehicle, let's get back to the road map and decide where we want to go in the future.

Think about the "big picture."

Ask yourself some important questions about what you want for your life.

The answers to this question can be as general as,

"I want to be happy knowing I always do my best."

Or

"I want to help inspire younger people involved in my chosen field/sport to do well also."

Or

*"I want to be remembered as one of the great ....
..................in years to come."*

These general statements can help home in on the things that really matter to you. Recognising the things you value will guide your decision-making and keep you focused on your end goals.

Think of the answers to your "big picture" questions as things you hope to attain 10, 15, or 20 years from now

Break the "big picture" down into smaller and more specific goals. Consider areas of your life that you either want to change or that you feel you would like to develop with time. Begin to ask yourself questions about what you'd like to achieve in each area of your life and how you would like to approach it within a one-to-five-year time-frame.

Look at your wheel of life and decide which area you need to work on and make stronger.

Use the SMART method to create actionable goals. SMART is a mnemonic used by life coaches and motivators for a system of goal identification, setting, and achievement.

Every letter in SMART stands for an adjective that describes an effective way to set goals.

- Specific - When setting goals, they should answer the highly specific questions of who, what, where, when, and why. Instead of the general goal, "I want to be better ....," try for a specific goal, "I want to qualify for my first ....this year."
- Measurable - In order for us to track our progress, goals should be quantifiable. "I'm going to practice more" is far more difficult to track and measure than "Everyday I'm going to practice for an extra 30 minutes."
- Attainable - It is important to evaluate your situation honestly and recognize which goals are realistic, and which are a little far-fetched. Instead of, "I am going to win a world title this year" it might be more realistic to say, "I am going to break my personal best which can take me to another step towards the world championships."

- Relevant - Is this goal relevant to your life and to the "big picture" questions you have already asked yourself?

Some good questions to ask yourself when figuring this out are:

- Does it seem worthwhile?
- Is now the right time for this?
- Does this match my needs?

Time-related

Setting a "due date" to meet goals not only keeps you on track, but it prevents pesky daily roadblocks from getting in the way.

Instead of saying, "I'm going to get my college degree."

You might consider saying, "I'm going to get my B.A. in 4 years."

Keep Track Of Your Progress

Journalling is a great way to keep track of personal progress. Checking in with yourself and acknowledging the progress made towards a certain goal is key to staying motivated.

Asking a friend in class with similar goals to buddy-up with you is a great way to keep you motivated and to make sure you hit your goal target dates also.

Reward Your Accomplishments

Acknowledge when you have reached goals and allow yourself to celebrate in your own way. Take this time to assess the goal process--from the start to completion.

If you feel it took too long to achieve this goal, examine your stumbling blocks. Was your goal reasonable? Are there skills you may need to acquire before attempting to complete other goals? Do you feel worth it?

If you learned something about the way you work towards meeting your goal, is it something that can be applied to other goals?

Are You Confident That You Can Get There?

Positive questions to help you become a better person and understand yourself more.

Ask yourself the questions that give you the answers to progress. What's more, keep a written record of your answers to these questions. It's easy for them to be forgotten in time.

If you have them written down, then you can review your notes and take it a step further, instead of answering the same questions all over again.

Keep them in a notebook that's both easy to access and update wherever you happen to be; it will be a source of sustenance for you, by which you can continue to measure your growth through life.

So Let's Get You Started

"If I had all the resources in the world what would I be doing with my day to day life and why?"

What do you want to look back on in your life and say that you never regretted?

Would you regret never having travelled abroad?

Would you regret never having auditioned for a part in a show, a trial for a team or even a promotion even if it meant risking rejection?

Would you regret not spending enough time with your family when you could?

This question can be difficult to answer so take your time as it is very important.

If you had to choose three words to describe the kind of person you would love to be, what would those words be?

Adventurous?

Loving?

Open?

Honest?

Hilarious?

Optimistic?

Don't be afraid to choose words that are considered negative because that proves you're a real person, and not a lopsided combination of parts other people want to be known for.

Sometimes the traits that you don't like become useful in dangerous situations (such as anger) for maybe dealing with a bully. Sometimes they are valuable to the job you're meant to perform correctly— like being fussy.

Who am I?

This question is not static. It should be one you continue to ask yourself throughout your life. A healthy person continues to reinvent themselves throughout their life.

By asking this question regularly, it updates your understanding of who you are and how you change. Instead of answering who you think you ought to be, keep it focused on who you are.

How would you answer this question?

Getting That Feeling Of "Yes, I Can!"

Like any feeling we experience as a human, confidence will fluctuate in different circumstances in our life. This is why it is important that you keep reminders around you that will bring back this feeling when you need it. Reminders such as books, personal notes and audio's.
Here is another exercise to keep cementing those building blocks of self-esteem and confidence.

Self Confidence Worksheet

Keep your completed self-esteem Worksheets handy. The next time you're feeling low self-esteem and need a self-esteem boost, read your Self Confidence worksheet and be reminded of your personal power and use it to transform situations in which you feel less confident.

PART ONE

Think of a situation in which you experienced confidence and a feeling of satisfaction and self-worth. Answer the following questions.

What were the situations?

What do you say to yourself about the situation (self talk)?

How do you feel physically? What sensations and feelings do you have in your body?

43

What did you do as a result of this?

Part Two

Think of a current situation in which you experienced a lack of confidence that you would like to change if you could.

What was the situation?

What do you say to yourself about the situation? (Self talk)

How do you feel physically?

What sensations and feelings do you have in your body?
What did you do as a result of this?

Part Three

Look at Part Two and using the information that you have learned about yourself in Part One, ask yourself:

When I am in this situation:

1. What positive statement could I say to myself to be reminded of my power?

2. What could I do that would help me feel differently? For example, create a visualisation in which I remember how I felt in Part One.

3. What could I do differently, next time I am in this situation?

4. What actions would empower me?

How To Avoid The Feeling Of "No I Can't!"

After taking the time to build self-confidence, many people break it down again unintentionally.

Why do some people lose confidence after experiencing a loss or setback?

Highly committed people, including perfectionists, hurt their confidence with a harsh attitude about the way they have performed.

Top performers know they must learn from their mistakes and poor performances so they can improve, which leads to improved confidence instead of self-doubt.

They don't become discouraged or feel helpless when they fail to win or do not perform up to their expectations. They are able to regroup by assessing their strengths and weaknesses.

The strength of your mental game has everything to do with the level of your confidence. You want to do everything in your power to grow your confidence and be your own best friend.

Three Tips To Stay Confident After A Poor Performance

1. Be more subjective about your performance - focus on a few things that went well and a few things you want to improve on.

2. Use mistakes as an opportunity to improve - make new goals and get motivation from what you've identified as needed improvements.

3. Give yourself credit for what you did well during your performance - don't just focus on mistakes, acknowledge the parts that went well.

Making A Self-Appreciation List

What makes you think you deserve all that you want to achieve in your life?

Is that a hard question to answer? Maybe you don't give yourself enough credit for all the things you are doing. Instead of thinking that you have to do all kinds of things in your daily life you might consider that you are a wonderful person that chooses to do them.

For it is a fact that nobody forces you to go to work, practice or study . You make that choice every single day for the benefit of yourself and others. Give yourself the credit of doing all those marvellous things each day that help you grow as a person and please your loved ones. Be proud of yourself in the same way that your parents and teachers were and are proud of you.

A great way of generating this feeling of appreciation for yourself, is to make an appreciation list.

Make your Appreciation List by starting each sentence with 'I am so proud of myself for...' Fill in every aspect of your life where you know you choose the right thing to do to contribute like 'I am so proud of myself for helping my Parents, friends, team or chosen charity.

'I am so proud of myself for writing this piece of work for school/ work group, although I wanted to listen to music instead. I am proud of myself for taking the time to cheer up a friend who was feeling sad. I am so proud of myself for working hard and getting the results my teacher/boss/coach knew I was capable of.

Go on and on until you feel a great sense of appreciation about yourself. Make sure you write or type the whole sentence starting with 'I am so proud of myself' for it will focus your attention on the feelings of pride. If you have a hard time finding things to be proud of, ask your parents/partner or a close friend to help you.

The Pleasure Is All Mine

The next time you are feeling unhappy take out your Pleasure List and do something on the list or imagine yourself doing something on the list. Then, notice your attitude change.

Shifting your focus, even for a moment, to something that you enjoy sends a clear message to your brain that says: "I deserve happiness." "I am in control of my thoughts and feelings." When you practice this activity you strengthen your self esteem muscle.

Make a List of the people and pets who bring a smile to your face when you think of them.

Make a List of the places that bring a smile to your face when you think of them.

Make a list of the things that bring a simile to your face when you think of them.

Make a list of the things you like to do that bring you pleasure.

Are You Beginning To Feel Better About Yourself?

More Confident, Happier?

Good! Let's keep building on this.

Toot Your Horn Work-list

Complete the statements underneath. If you cannot answer an item, don't worry - simply complete what you can.

Keep your completed Self Esteem Worksheets handy.

The next time you're feeling low self esteem and need a boost read your Toot Your Horn worksheet and remind yourself of your natural resources and personal power.

- I like myself because:

- I'm an expert at:

- I feel good about:

- My friends would tell you I have a great:

- My favourite activity is:

- I'm loved by:

- People say I am a good:

- I've been told I have pretty:

- I consider myself a good:

- What I enjoy most is:

- The people I admire the most are:

- I have a natural talent for:

- Goals for my future are:

- I know I will reach my goals because I am:

- People compliment me about:

- I feel good when I:

- I've been successful at:

- I laugh when I think about:

- The traits I admire myself for are:

- I feel peaceful when:

- What are your thoughts and feelings about yourself after completing and contemplating these questions?

Knowing Your Values

Our values are those important rules that will live by and make decisions on, even when we are not aware of them. When you are aware of your own values you have gained a great source of self-knowledge that can help you make decisions and give you direction in your life. You will also be aware of what activities you should avoid if they do not co-exist with your values.

A List Of Life Values

Choose 10 that appeal to you the most, then prioritise your top five. Then number from 1 to 5 in order of importance to you.

These values should be a part of your ideal lifestyle and achievement statements for the future to make sure that you are living a life that matches your values.

For example, if your values where caring, success, helping, control and discovery, you could put these in a paragraph of how you would like to be in the future such as:

"I want to be a great athletic coach in the future known for my caring, controlled style of teaching that will focus on skills as well as discovering new things about myself that will help my students develop in their life, and give me that feeling of success."

Value List

Adventure - Activities that are new and different for you.

Aesthetics - Appreciating or studying the beauty of ideas, surroundings or objects.

Attractiveness - The appearance of yourself and others.

Belonging - And being accepted as a worthwhile member of a group.

Caring - Showing and compassion.

Helping - Those in need.

Career - Achieving success in chosen field of work.

Challenging Problems - Engaging in complex questions and demanding tasks.

Community - Being part of a supportive community of people.

Competition - And participating in activities that pit personal skills and abilities against others.

Connectedness - Being close and connected to others.

Conformity - Acting and behaving within social norms.

Control - Being in command of your environment and surroundings.

Cooperation - Working and acting towards a common end or purpose.

Creative Expression - Expressing your ideas in novel and unique ways. Having the opportunity for experimentation and innovation.

Discovery - Exploring and identifying new approaches to the world.

Diversity - Appreciating differences in people, ideas, and situations.

Family - Building and maintaining a close-knit family.

Fairness - Demonstrating a commitment to justice and the equal treatment of individuals.

Fidelity - Being faithful and loyal to family and friends.

Health - Maintaining a healthy body and mind.

Honesty - Demonstrating truthfulness and sincerity.

Humility - Demonstrating modesty in behaviour, attitude, and spirit.

Independence - Determining a course of action free from control by others.

Influence - Being able to change attitudes or beliefs of other people.

Knowledge - Engaging in the pursuit of scholarship, truth and understanding.

Leadership - Having the ability to motivate and inspire others towards a common vision.

Loyalty - Being steadfast in allegiance to people, ideals or customs.

Luxury - Enjoying the richness of comforts and pleasures.

Nature - Enjoyment of the outdoors. Honouring nature.

Passion - Feelings of excitement and connection to people, purpose and activities.

Personal Growth - Advancing and progressing in mind, body and spirit throughout life.

Pleasure - Seeking satisfaction, sensual gratification and fun.

Pursuit of Excellence - Performing tasks to the best of your ability.

Recognition - Seeking positive feedback and acceptance for well-done tasks.

Respect - Recognising others' worth and right to self-determination.

Responsibility - Demonstrating ethical accountability for decisions and actions.

Risk-taking - Aspiring to the difficult, challenging and sometimes impossible.

Security - Being free from fear, danger, or risk, to exist in a stable environment.

Self-Interest - Having high regard for personal interests and advantages.

Sensitivity - Being aware of and sensitive to the needs and wants of others.

Service - Contributing to and being involved in efforts to help individuals or groups without motive or personal gain.

Simplicity - Enjoying a simple, non complex and excessive life.

Spirituality - Having awareness of the connection to a higher power, a world view that includes a higher purpose and meaning.

Status - Gaining the respect of others.

Success Personal and professional lifelong achievement.

Tolerance - Recognising and respecting the opinions, practices and behaviours of others.

Trustworthiness - Fulfilling commitments and keeping promises.

Wealth - Accumulating enough material possessions and money to free yourself from worry.

Variety - Finding frequent change of activities and settings.

See It, Believe It, Achieve It!!

Some Powerful reasons to use visualisation as part of your strategy to achieve your goals.

Mental practice can get you closer to where you want to be in life, and it can prepare you for success! For instance, Natan Sharansky, a computer specialist who spent 9 years in prison in the USSR after being accused of spying for the US has a lot of experience with mental practices. While in solitary confinement, he played himself in mental chess, saying: "I might as well use the opportunity to become the world champion!" Remarkably, in 1996, Sharansky beat world champion chess player Garry Kasparov!

A study looking at brain patterns in weightlifters found that the patterns activated when a weightlifter lifted hundreds of pounds were similarly activated when they only imagined lifting.

An exercise psychologist from Cleveland Clinic Foundation in Ohio, compared "people who went to the gym with people who carried out virtual workouts in their heads". He found that a 30% muscle increase in the group who went to the gym. However, the group of participants who conducted mental exercises of the weight training increased muscle strength by almost half as much (13.5%). This average remained for 3 months following the mental training.

Tiger Woods who has been using it since his pre-teen years. Seasoned athletes use vivid, highly detailed internal images and run-through of the entire performance, engaging all their senses in their mental rehearsal, and they combine their knowledge of the sports venue with mental rehearsal.

World Champion Golfer Jack Nicklaus has said: "I never hit a shot, not even in practice, without having a very sharp in-focus picture of it in my head".

Even heavyweight champion, Muhammad Ali, used different mental practices to enhance his performance in the ring such as: "affirmation; visualisation; mental rehearsal; self-confirmation; and perhaps the most powerful affirmation of personal worth ever uttered: "I am the greatest".

Tips:

Use all 5 Senses in Your Visualisation

Despite its name, visualisation should include more than just your eyesight. Imagine with all of your senses that what you dream is a reality. See the image in your mind's eye, hear the sounds, taste it, smell it, and feel it in your body.

1. Get Dramatic and Act Out Your Visualisation.

Be playful and use your imagination. Role-play is a great technique for kinaesthetic (Feeling) learners. Acting out your visualisation will help you feel in your body that your dreams are already a reality.

If it helps, have a partner act with you. For example, if you are trying to manifest a role in a professional show as a dancer, have a partner pretend to be your lead dancer. The two of you can act out the show.

Close your eyes and imagine you are receiving a reward in a massive venue, preparing for a radio interview, rehearsing, smashing your personal best records in sport. The only limit with visualisation is the one you put on it.

2. Use Props

Props are a great way to trick the unconscious mind into believing something is reality.

Actor Jim Carrey grew up in a poor family and would often dream of being an actor. He took his visualisations seriously and would imagine directors coming up to him and offering him acting jobs.

Jim is famous for using props in his visualisations. He once wrote himself a check for 10 million dollars, dated it a few years in advance, and wrote, "for acting services rendered" in the memo line. Just a few months before the check date, he received 10 million dollars for his role in Dumb & Dumber.

Be creative when using props. But, make them seem as realistic as possible. For example, if you are trying to manifest getting a role in a show or winning an Olympic medal, practice receiving the medal or wear similar costumes to those performers in the show when practicing at home.

3. Meditate Immediately Prior to Visualisation

Meditation will put you in a relaxed open state, which allows your visualisation to penetrate you on a deeper level. Relaxing the mind will help silence your mind and clear out any negative thoughts, beliefs, fears, and doubts that will hold you back from achieving your goals.

4. Visualise Several Times a Day

The more you visualise, the better. Use moments of down time to practice short 2 to 3 minute visualisations.

5. Write Your Visualisations Down

Write your visualisations down using descriptive language. The memory system responds well to the written word and this will reinforce the ideas in your mind, particularly if you have a visual learning style.

6. Create a Vision Board

A vision board will make your visualisation tangible. Use photographs, magazine cut-outs, and other items to create a vision board of your goal. Look at it frequently to remind you of that which you hope to accomplish.

7. Be Within Your Own Limits

For best results, start out visualising that which is believable to you. Once you start seeing results, then you may find that you are able to stretch your limits even further after seeing the true creative power you hold in your life.

8. Be Proactive

Jim Carrey once stated on the Oprah Show, "Visualisation works if you work hard. That's the thing.

Visualisation is not magic.

You still have to put in effort when trying to achieve a goal. I hope that you find these visualisation strategies effective at manifesting what you want in your life.

Each of us possesses a unique and creative source of infinite potential within us. Unlock yours by retraining your brain and releasing your limiting beliefs, fears, and doubts that hold you back.

Unlock Your Mind

Harry Houdini the legendary magician, illusionist and escape artist was famous for escaping from prisons, submerged trunks, bank vaults, and jumping off bridges into rivers covered in ice.

For example, in one of his most famous and spectacular feats, he broke out of Scotland Yard, even though one of the conditions of the challenge was that he be allowed NO clothing whatsoever — in order to keep him from concealing tools or keys.

So how did he do it?

Quite simple, really. Using a razor blade, he cut a small, invisible slit in a heavy callous on his heel. Under this tiny flap of hardened skin, he concealed a small piece of watch spring. Then, once he was alone, he used this little strip of metal to pick all the locks. He then tossed the tool away and walked out!

Looking to capitalise on Houdini's immense popularity and fame, a London bank challenged him to break out of their vault with its new, state-of-the-art locking system. They were CERTAIN that even the great Houdini would finally meet his match.

Houdini accepted, and on the appointed date, the press turned out in droves to see if the master could get out in the three and a half minutes allotted.

This time he got to keep his clothes on. But he had another trick up his sleeve! His contracts always specified that before he disappeared into the trunk or cell or behind a small curtain (when performing on a stage), he could kiss his wife. After all, many of his feats were seriously dangerous, so who could refuse the couple what might turn out to be their last goodbye?

But what no one knew was that he was getting more than a kiss! As their lips met, his wife would secretly pass a small piece of wire from her mouth to his. Then, once he was alone or hidden behind the curtain, he'd use the wire to pick the locks.

This time out, though, the wire didn't seem to be doing the trick. Here's what Houdini wrote about that experience:

"After one solid minute, I didn't hear any of the familiar clicking sounds. I thought, my gosh, this could ruin my career, I'm at the pinnacle of fame, and the press is all here.

After two minutes, I was beginning to sweat profusely because I was not getting this lock picked. After three minutes of failure, with thirty seconds left, I inadvertently reached into my pocket to get a handkerchief and dry my hands and forehead, and when I did, I leaned against the vault door and it creaked open."

And there you have it, my friend. The door was never locked! But because Harry BELIEVED it to be locked, it might as well have been. Only the "accident" of leaning on the door changed that belief and saved his career.

It's the same way with all of us. The things we believe to be insurmountable barriers, obstacles, and problems are just like the bank vault door. The only lock is in our minds, and if we simply believe that we CAN'T, well, we can't.
But when we give the door a push, we can be amazed to find that not only is the door not locked to us, but there's also really no door at all, just the illusion of one.

We can all be master magicians. All we must do is face whatever barrier seems to be looming before us, then take the first step, give the door a shove. The biggest obstacles are the ones we have created ourselves in our minds, and when we give our focus, faith, and feeling to them, THEY become our vision — and then they become real.

How To Become Successful In Achieving Your Goals

It matters not if your main goal is just to feel great with my GREAT process or to become great in some avenue of your life you will need to follow a strategy.

The Ps of success are steps of a strategy that have been used from the beginning of time by human beings to achieve success in their chosen field.

This chapter is a little reminder for you in case you have forgotten this powerful method that you once used in childhood to master so many hundreds of skills. Read this chapter when you feel you are losing some ground on yourself.

Make the Ps of success yours again to keep and pass on to those who you think could do with a bit of a boost! I hope you enjoy this chapter as much as I enjoyed writing it for you.

Preparation makes the difference between winning and losing, surviving, or being eliminated. It is a vital ingredient for success. But how many times do we just stumble into things in life without proper preparation. Preparation is all but forgotten by most adults who become complacent with their surroundings in life. They take on a challenge in a state of worry, fear, or insecurity. They are doomed before they begin. What chance do you have if you begin a task feeling small with self-doubt and no confidence in yourself?

Every cell in your body knows what you are thinking and will react accordingly to the energy of that thought process. So how should you prepare yourself?

Well, let's look back to when you were a child about to embark on the challenge of walking, riding a bicycle or skipping.

Where did the motivation come from?

Well, where does human motivation come from?

Let's take an example:

If I asked you to do a task for me, something that you do not like to do, where would your motivation be on a scale of 1- 10.

You will need to close your eyes for this exercise and go inside to notice how you feel when you think of a task that you do not particularly like.

Now close your eyes and imagine that if I told you if you performed the task really well there would be a holiday, somewhere you would really enjoy, with spending money for you.

Where would you be on that 1-10 scale now?

Has the penny dropped yet?

Humans only do something if they feel, see, or hear a result that will make them feel better. If someone tells you they would like more money, a new car, a new house, job or even a makeover, what they are really saying is if I had that, I think I would feel better. The better the feelings and benefits you can associate to you reaching your result the more chance you will have of reaching it.

People

We can only get so far in life without people. And believe me, that is not very far. So, who are these people we need so much?

Well, family and friends for love and support, that is obvious. Doctors, nurses, dentists to help keep us out of pain and danger, mechanics to look after our transport. Shop assistants to find those shoes for the big night out. The taxi driver that takes you home, so you needn't bring the car.

We take so many people for granted these days but without them we would lead a difficult life. Plumbers, electricians, police, bricklayers, and even parking inspectors. Oh, and let's not forget the people who have already achieved what you are working towards. They can give you valuable knowledge that will help you along your path.

Practice This: The P of all Ps

This Is How To Master Life Itself. Practice.

The secret of all secrets of success. You show me the best athletes in the world, and I will show you the ones who put in the most practice. The greatest businessmen, speakers and skilled trade's men improve by practice.

There are four stages to mastery of any skill.

1. Unconscious Incompetence
We don't know that we don't know.
An energetic two-year-old boy wants to ride a bike that he sees his older brother riding. But he doesn't know that he doesn't know how to ride it. Most of us in business who have never had extensive feedback about our interpersonal skills are in this state of unconscious incompetence.

2. Conscious Incompetence
We know that we don't know.
Here we learn that we are not competent at something. This often comes as a rude awakening. The two-year-old boy gets on a bike and falls off. He has immediately gone from stage one to stage two and knows that he does not know how to ride a bike.

3. Conscious Competence
We work at what we don't know.
Here we consciously try to learn a new skill. Practice, drill and repetition are at the forefront. This is where most learning takes place. It takes effort and work. The little boy carefully steers and balances and pedals and thinks of what he is doing, step by step.

4. Unconscious Competence
We don't have to think about knowing it.
Here the skill set happens automatically at an unconscious level. The little boy rides his bike without even thinking about it. He can whistle, talk, sing, or do other things with his mind at the

same time. Another example that we can all probably relate to is driving a car.

The key is to recognise where you are at in the 4 stages of learning and be patient with yourself.

Every skill you begin to learn you will have to go through the four stages if you wish to gain mastery.

Unfortunately, most adults give up at the first stage because it can feel clumsy, uncomfortable and they believe that others are judging their performance.

If you yourself fall into this category I suggest that you remind yourself that you have passed through this stage many thousands of times in your life when learning new skills. All you must do to pass through this stage is to fit in more hours of practice. Simple!

So always remind yourself that no-one is better than you at anything in this life. They just have practiced longer. Give the great achievers respect, but do not get into the trap of looking up to them. If you are always looking up to people you will feel lower or beneath them and you are as good as anyone on this earth.

Persistence

"Much rain wears the marble." (Shakespeare) This must be my favourite quote. Everything will finally give way if you are persistent enough. A steady quiet persistence is superior to the persistence of a door salesman or a child wanting sweets in a supermarket. Move forward gradually, continuing to grow in your knowledge, and always focus on your end result. If you lose sight of your end goal your persistence will fade away into the darkness.

Develop the persistence you possessed as an infant when you embarked on your journey to master the skill of walking.

Progression

If you are persistent in your practice with the right people and mental preparation plus do not lose patience with yourself, you will surely improve and progress along the path.

Progression, no matter how small, should always be rewarded. Human beings need recognition for their achievements. This makes them feel good about themselves and appreciate themselves. When we were all children, we achieved and mastered hundreds of skills and this was partly to do with our parents giving us verbal and material rewards for recognition.

Sadly, we enter the adult world and people are so busy with their own life that they do not always remember to praise you for your efforts. That is why so many people lose heart; they begin to think 'why bother, why put the effort in, no one cares anyway'. Therefore, it is so important to reward yourself verbally and materially. Keep records of your progression to remind yourself of how you are continuing to grow. When you look at it in black and white you will naturally feel good about yourself.

So, well done to you for everything you have achieved in your life up to this point. Be proud of yourself because you have mastered many skills and overcame many obstacles. From learning to walk, talk, sing, write, cycle, swim, negotiate, job skills, overcoming pain, injury, grief and so much more.

Pleasure

Never has there been such a driver for human performance as pleasure. Most of us will not make the effort for any goal unless inside our head we associate pleasure to the end result.

When we get asked to perform a task for someone, in a fraction of a second, we feel the end result associated with pleasure, pain or boredom. We actually feel many experiences before we analytically work it out.

So think about a task that you have been putting off. Then close your eyes and notice how you feel about this task. Feels uncomfortable, doesn't it? Now close your eyes again. Think of all the benefits with good feelings at the end of this task. Make them big, think about how good you will feel after the effort, and how you found this motivation and personal power inside yourself to complete the task. Did you notice a difference in how you felt the second time?

We tend to behave like a stubborn donkey when it comes to certain tasks in life. Push that donkey and pull it and notice how stubborn it becomes but produce a couple of carrots in front of it and off it goes.

Well for you my friend, pleasure of some kind and it is usually emotional, is the carrot that you should have at the end result of any task. So, if you find that you have lost the drive to complete a task, first put lots of pleasure and benefits at the end result. You have been given an imagination so use it to motivate yourself.

Positive Mental Attitude

You could read thirty books on how to adapt a positive mental attitude and still fall back into your old negative attitude. Too many books complicate the lesson they are trying to get across which is why we never put them into use. Life is complicated enough. Keep it simple and you will keep it. That has always been my approach.

I mentioned earlier in this book that all anybody really wanted was a state of mind. Well, developing a positive mental attitude will give you just that. It is not always easy but with practice you can make it habitual. It is simple. Is the glass half empty or half full? You decide.

If you see it as half empty, you are right, if you see it as half full you are also right. There are only two ways to look at anything in life. If I fail at my first attempt at a task I can complain, get angry, blame others and not try again (half empty). OR I can look at it as an opportunity to see where I need to strengthen certain skills and put it down to a learning experience that I can use in the future (half full).

I leave the office to find my car has been hit by a lorry side on. I can get angry with the driver (half empty) or I can give thanks that I was not getting into it or that a child was beside it (half full). It won't change the state of my car but neither will getting annoyed.

Some people we meet in this world see everything as half empty. When they enter a room of strangers, they look for things they do not like. They won't like your accent, your hair, clothes, your friends, your views, how you laugh or where you live. Then there are the other people who when they enter a room they will look for things that they like in people. They are full of curiosity instead of criticism and tend to take everyone just as they are.

Which one of these categories do you fall into?

Prayer

From the beginning of time, in every country, in every language, humans have used some sort of prayer for help. It is probably the oldest strategy for help around. So, to me that means it must be working or why would people continue to use it? Now there are many theories on religion and how it should be practiced and of course everyone thinks theirs is the best. This is natural. Use what works for you and what feels right. One thing I personally avoid is asking for too many things in prayer.

This tends to make you feel as if you are always in need. It will make you feel better if you just give thanks for all that you have received. This gives the feeling of appreciation and contentment.

Gratitude is such a phenomenal feeling and science has even recognised the powerful effect of gratitude on our health and performance.

Medical research explains how the heart responds to emotional and mental reactions and why certain emotions stress the body and drain our energy.

As we experience feelings like anger, frustration, anxiety and insecurity, our heart-rhythm patterns become more erratic. These erratic patterns are sent to the emotional centres in the brain, which recognizes them as negative, or stressful feelings. These signals create the actual feelings we experience in the heart area and elsewhere in the body. Erratic heart rhythms also block our ability to think clearly.

Conversely, research shows, when we experience heartfelt emotions such as gratitude, love, care and compassion, the heart produces a very different rhythm –which is indicative of positive emotions, to be indicators of cardiovascular efficiency and nervous-system balance. This lets the brain know the heart feels good; often we experience this as a gentle, warm feeling in the area of the heart. Learning to shift out of stressful emotional reactions to these heartfelt emotions can have profound positive effects on our cardiovascular systems and overall health.

So, I guess this concludes the Great book with it's simple yet powerful strategies to help you feel great and for some of you to eventually become great in your chosen field.

Remember to study and apply this book throughout your life.

There is no point in just reading a book such as this once and then putting it away.

Study it and memorise the words until they become engrained deep within your mind.

I wish you the reader success on your terms, inner happiness, and balanced health well into your future.

Best regards.
Sean.

For more information or to inquire on how you may work with Sean, contact us at

seanconnollylive@gmail.com

Personal Notes

Personal Notes

Printed in Great Britain
by Amazon